Yoga for Pickpockets

Mike Silverton

Sagging Meniscus

Set in Mrs Eaves XL with LaTeX.

ISBN: 978-1-952386-99-2 (paperback)
Library of Congress Control Number: 2024935656

Sagging Meniscus Press
Montclair, New Jersey
saggingmeniscus.com

I dedicate this collection to Jim Heanue (Graham Fundible), who introduced a young man to Surrealism's bent antics, to Bill Cole, who included my work in four of his anthologies, to my wife Lee for her loving support, and most emphatically to my publisher, Jacob Smullyan.

Contents

YOGA FOR PICKPOCKETS

Art

Art sniffs out apfelstrudel from which no one
takes comfort—a setting more resembling confectionery
slime whereon cliques collide.
Pip! Pap! Pop! Aargh!
This cannot—must not—stand!

Well yes, but so long ago
when almost everyone produced insightful delights.
Seated on ice cubes, sphincters benumbed,
aesthetes flourished.

A loving couple consume a phantom feast,
masticating their way to an even longer-ago,
and on the horizon a twilight's droopy eyelid, so no,
this horizon holds no promise.

Boring Art natters on about this and that.
Interesting Art rarely settles for bland outcomes.
The Best Art leaves us at the starting gate.
So yes, reader, prenez garde!

The Regent

The Regent holds court in a vat of cock-a-leekie.
The Regent prefers cock-a-leekie's odor to that of borscht.
The Regent mistakes cock-a-leekie stasis for spirituality.
The Regent's spontaneity resembles cock-a-leekie squirts.

The Regent's proximity-fuzed door prizes imperil a fragile détente.
The Regent's travelogue, Meine Stinken Fahrt, contains not a single umlaut!
The Regent delivers his regret-face address at his weekly auto da fé.
The Regent pokes about under the bushel where his light is said to be hidden.

The Regent's edicts in Proto-Welsh are curiously entertaining.
The Regent demands of his mirror, Who gave you permission to wear my face?
The Regent's ball gown and hour-glass figure lead to confusion.
The Regent declines invitations to events requiring batteries.

The Regent remains indoors when the heavens shed shards.
The Regent's dispensations are mistaken for calliope toots.
The Regent says, I give them iron lungs. Does anyone thank me?
The Regent applies palette-knife textures to his generals' battle plans.

The Regent's abundant opinions rattle when he walks.
The Regent thinks of something else he should have said.
The Regent welcomes the palace's first penguins.
The Regent, had he wished it, could roll up your lawn.

The Regent whispers state secrets to trustworthy furnishings.
The Regent enjoys pushing red buttons.
The Regent's parents spoke in reverse to spare his feelings.
The Regent favors edible transitions.

The Regent's occasional evaporations cast doubt on his resolve.
The Regent believes an aspic is a toothpick's anal counterpart.
The Regent turned Cousin Lewis into an asparagus.
The Regent encourages moonlit calligraphy.

The Regent calls for plonk and any available thou when he reads the Rubaiyat.
The Regent's peppermint alpenstock resembles a candy cane.
The Regent asks the Tooth Fairy which dental products she recommends.
The Regent thinks Stabat Mater means Stop That, Mother (*pace* Pergolesi).

The Regent preserves his best memories in Formalin.
The Regent's ice cubes embody the essence of evanescence.
The Regent avoids targets that shoot back.
The Regent notes that, from above, his forests look like broccoli.

The Regent mislaid his velvet fist's iron glove.
The Regent receives raptors but only after they've dined.
The Regent has been informed that turning the other cheek is not a tropism.
The Regent's clouds wipe their noses on his shoulder.

The Regent favors vacuum cleaners for removing small petitioners.
The Regent, when he babbles, demands to know whose tongue occupies his
    mouth.
The Regent perforce wears his kepi to bed, having failed at biting it off.
The Regent's pubic lice find contentment in long walks.

The Regent pelts adulterers with dust bunnies he harvests from under their beds.
The Regent's bon mots amuse his parrot.
The Regent investigates every sparrow's fall with respect to residency.
The Regent's three sheets to the wind account for missing bed linens.

The Regent's revanchist dandelions encroach on neighboring gardens.
The Regent, astride his grand mare, Grand Mare, reviews the realm's nursing
    homes.
The Regent regards constipation as fecal sedition.
The Regent slips out at night through rifts in the alphabet.

Benedict Arnold

Drink the paint, Benedict. The color suits you.
In your special kind of moonlight,
how difficult to parse your treachery
with your shirt pulled over your face. Even so,
imagine rocks everywhere, rocks, rocks and more rocks.
And over there, a restive cavalry
as black as your heart.

On May 10, 1869, some years after the traitor's passing (June 14, 1801),
a golden spike is driven home at Promontory Point, Utah.
In era-appropriate attire, draped on and around their locomotives,
the railroad men bask in satisfaction.
(The tricorn is long passé.)

Benedict's carotid artery throbs.
There follows a snow that masks a fraught moment.

If your attention wanders but for an instant,
Benedict will rearrange your belongings.
A man of taste withal, Benedict's wallpaper
features garnet-stuffed squirrels.

Benedict stops at the door and collapses, exhausted.
His mother mistakes him for a dog she hates.
"Open, sesame! Look, I'm smiling! I have soapy eyes
and a cracked flat nose."

Benedict's epaulettes dangle and swing,
embroidered pendulums, now here, now there.
He walks his stallion past mounds of swooned ladies.

Benedict's treachery flows from a hole in his head.
He fosters an illusion of a drawbridge in the fog.
Even dragons decline to attack.

As do we, Benedict displaces a measure of emptiness
with a presence he's been cultivating since birth.

Benedict is folding money. A little dog seems interested
in the hat Benedict wears for shady events.
And now comes third-cousin Otto returning Benedict's lawn mower.

Yes, reader, we fritter away a life – and poof!
Ha! Wouldn't it be something if Otto rose up from the grave and said,
"I don't like it here!" Benedict weeps. He burns with treachery and hate
yet we see him striding to the defense of whatever requires defending.
Similarly, surveying a fairyland, Otto dies again.
Otto seems, newly dead, Mr. Peanut's twin.
The tears that Benedict sheds taste like mayonnaise.

Mourners cluster at a pier, all chatty froth and bubbles.
They look like a shampoo. Flying squirrels inspire Benedict,
taking his leisure under lindens, to emerge with plans
for an aircraft to bust the foe's cajones.
How like a movie! Invisible trombones pump and chomp!
Benedict: "Just now, rodents, I steeped you in my genius and added propellers."

Benedict, what does Chairman Mao say regarding your expensive blond father?
Benedict's batman is lost somewhere in the flower flops.

Think of it, Benedict! A mighty fleet of men o' war,
some as long as boring poems!

Like fescue on Benedict's manhood, Fortuna embraces a lime-green personage,
palace protocols, this how-do-you-call-it, to terrorize the irresolute
with brains in the fatuous acorn pattern.

As mama used to say, think before you roll yourself into a ball and throw yourself
        away.
Ich bin der geist von Madame Blavatsky! Give the money to the monkey! Phew!
It's only Benedict's mama coming out of the closet.

Benedict shouts, "Promise you won't forget me!"
He gathers flowers for his hair, wakes the birds, grabs one, is airborne,
is known soon after as the singing traitor,
in and out of view.

Saint Cloud

The legend of Saint Cloud,
picking his way through colleagues' relics,
arriving at spontaneity, saying out loud, No, really,
I should be in Heaven, and so he does it—he enters Heaven,
grafts his tongue to his chin, tries to sing.
But lacks the stamina. (As to flagging stamina,
couples who begin a beguine pause to inspect a reverie.)

Katana-wielding assassins favor invisible jodhpurs.
Their victims' flight through snow calls Saint Cloud to mind.

Saint Cloud is treated for asthma (yoga for pickpockets).

Saint Cloud clings to concavities
so as not to alert the extrovert element.
St. Cloud hones his katana.
It is foolish to relax.

Sinister Poets

Sinister poets abduct Mrs. Superman. Land o'Goshen! Banzai!
Sinister poets underscore their demands with the blood of poets they don't like.
Sinister poets spirit Mrs. Superman across stately lines.
Explosions follow close behind. "Not our fault!"
Blue skies, blue eyes, Eddie Rickenbacker, immelmanning butterflies.
Mrs. Superman remarks an odor. Nostalgia?
Sinister poets will not hear of it, question her sanity.
"My destiny promises punctures and precipitous decline."
"Nay! Not so!" cry sinister poets. "Let us, rather, nip your mind's skin
with the midges of our wit. Let us, rather, do the twitchy thing,
which it pleases us to call our Monroe Doctrine.
Let us arrive at a peaceful conclusion in the silence of the page.
We would like to love you."

For a Funny Man

You are a funny man.
You look like my underwear
or a bale of cotton with eyes
or shit on my shirt
or him who scurries about with my fingers
or the actor who offers nothing
or a flashy rabbi with a sore throat
or a sagging wall
or the girl who broke my nose
or the man who sits on my arm
or the man who waves goodbye to children
or a bundle of earth
or a game leg
or the Kremlin
or the stool which, if it could walk,
would limp.

&

& my poems' subtexts honor sea otters, belly up, sighing,
O salty waters, whither our porpoise? If a swain's poems fall short
of their purpose, he had best install a finger in the beloved's nostril. (Either one.)

& the young surgeon shakes his fist at the dawn: "How dare you reveal
Granny Philomel's eczema! Roll backward into the night!"

& je t'adore sounds like shut the door. On what?
On whom? I doubt I'm the first to remark the confusion.

& an ingot dragged across a replica waterfall sounds like
squealing blackboard chalk. Further aperçu to follow.

& birds and trees mature and expire at velocities consistent
in their difference. We include mine shafts. In keeping
with the pace of more collegial times, battles should conclude with
a performance of Wellington's Victory, the shaking of hands
and popping of balloons.

& poetry should be more engaging than wallpaper.
Similarities spell trouble—not to disrespect walls or indeed paper,
which fall among legitimate interests. On an uneventful Wednesday,
a poet rolls home in patterned lengths.

& as a test of authenticity, stand the applicant in sunlight
and look for signs of dissolution.

& depart through a windshield. Your faith will attend
to your wounds. If you must spit, do it on Ash Wednesday
and aim for my forehead.

& I find myself staring, perhaps at a ghost.
It's difficult to be sure with one's shirt pulled up
over one's face.

Opera Poem

Opera isn't so much about what a hero, heroine or villain does
as in how he, she, it or they feel before, during and after an action.
When Phall learns that Vulv has departed via trebuchet to who knows where
his thoughts turn to rescue. However,
rather than dashing off as one would in what we call real life,
he steps forward and sings of his mad desire for vengeance.

Aria: "Away to autumn's bunting, mulchy, sodden Fate! Vulv outrages endures
as scene 'pon scene slips from view away, seven (7) clams remaining,
seven static, stoical clams."

Follow-up aria: "Tell me of Vulv one more time, again please."
It shows as only music can that Phall's love is genuine,
and that she, the diva, has given him her heart,
exclusive of aorta, liver slivers and dollops of spleen.

Stage left: Gypsies enter, feasting on acorns and rabbit debris,
quaffing grappa and bursting into waggish song,
"I shake your hand, now count your fingers."
And whilst our principal wonders aloud, "Could she be in this zany mob?"
his visage encounters a coconut-cream pie. What a funny indignity!
Interest shifts to fresh Gypsies hauling female acquisitions.
Ensemble: "This is your (our) dwelling now."

Where budgetary constraints apply, with top-shelf voices in short supply,
imagination's the thing. Imagine: Whilst milling about a bazaar,
Phall pauses to admonish a layabout. The lights dim, the layabout curses his fate.
This is opera. You're asked to believe.

For example, suppose a vermin loses incentive. Slinks away into its lair.
Just suppose. It costs you nothing. There is, as you've agreed to suppose, a
        beautiful queen—
princess really, possibly bogus—off at a distance. Behind a gauzy screen. Backlit.
        Weeping.
Her ladies in waiting cajole, plead, sing ditties, tell naughty jokes,
hop about with bright eyes flashing, getting nowhere.

As an event, a packaged entertainment, as tunes you hum as you leave the opera
    house,
a weeping queen is a simultaneity, a stylized occupation of time,
much like a portrait hovering midair.
Its fascination includes the likelihood of falling, damaging the elaborate frame.
Conversely, in opera, when we cannot see anything, much less hear it,
we fail to grasp its raisin debit. This failure to grasp an unheard event's raisin
    debit
might well be interpreted as a longing to embrace a metaphysical speculation.

The audience is adrift. One speaks of an ideal state.
The diva creates legends, topographical features even!
The diva is adrift. She recedes with the tide. She returns on a wave of expectation,
of wild carbonation!—the spirit of Schweppes or maybe spumante!
And so 'tis finally fixed, an unqualified abundance.

Meanwhile, a fop. Well, not exactly. Elsewhere puts it better.
A dandy. Homesick. Nostalgic. Drenched in sentimentality. Waterlogged.
The opera made it so. He recalls high teas, men's-room assignations,
the focus knob he fusses with, awaiting the diva.
His companions die. The cash in his billfold is no longer valid.
The heart he carved in the old oak tree a cardio-vascular network became.

Desire

1.

departing in slivers

tossing sparks
(the lover's ignition)

2.

nor guests
exiting hastily

nor vegans
dining epically

3.

nor featured in a poem
like a misapplied grommet

nor among ingredients
more injured than injurious

4.

nor peeling paint
resembling jujubes dropping off shelves

"The more sated the crotch,
the greater the itch."

Boric Acid

An aviator sets out to skywrite BORIC ACID.
Cruise ship passengers observe his plane glinting in the sunlight
as he banks to emit letters of smoke.
Passenger: Is he writing BORIC ACID?
Passenger: Maybe. Hard to tell.

A deliveryman who cannot say why
screams Boric acid! at a housewife.

A mounted moose head in a dimly lit tavern
bears the legend Boric Acid etched on an oval brass plate.

A SWAT team greets liberated hostages with shouts of Boric acid!
along with snappy salutes of index fingers to brows.

Daybreak. Borek A-Cid emerges from his yurt.
Moments later he buries his face,
furrowed by anguish, in embroidered throw pillows.

August Poem

Gustav Fabergé is lost in thought with a half-dozen eggs,
"Weeping urchins hanging off eaves, smelling like something."

O my swan, how, absent handles, shall we proceed?
(How, too, absent directions?)
An urchin knocks.
"Gentle door, open, O please do!
No no! I eat so little!"

And the sun, especially yellow that late afternoon,
fulfills a deathbed wish.

Asterisks, fungi, a hint of snails
a voice whisp'ing "Pillage!"
Expressionless mammals standing in snow,
who speaks for them?

That would be me, recalling trysts.
One finds me on tenterhooks,
muttering a leave-taking including bagged edibles.

Sensing no further despondencies, I decommission
and decompose.

Our Hearts Go Out

Our hearts go out to the underdog
until he vomits on the children. We insist on nausea
with tact! Mother had an adage: Never roll yourself into a wad.
People are likely to mistake you for trash.

Cow parsnip! father exclaims,
pointing through the windshield lately shattered
in the recent collision. Let us locate a fog within which to bemoan
anyone's passing. Weep loudly, mourners!
Confuse the birds.

Recent finding: psoriatic aesthetics was the cause of dragon extinction.
Also slapping them on their snouts.
They didn't like that. (Our hearts go out.)

I was one of several children sitting in water,
a soon-to-be poet patiently hydrating.
Our hearts go out as often as not through the wrong faucet.
To martyrs for example. Or my style,
perhaps best described as ne'er-do-well diction
on the court-house steps of a small Mississippi town
on a hot and humid afternoon.

Quintessence

When the Poet awakens snakes slither and weasels creep,
on the prowl for plats de jour.
And the Poet sets out to restore his Quintessence.
(Hello again, Mystic Rose!)

Automata arrive in vermillion robes,
vanish in a stand of lifelike Christmas trees,
and no longer figure in this narrative.

The Poet goes by many names.
Untrustworthy Lever.
Spring-Loaded Vacancy.
Permanently Clammy.
Ignoring Mama, Running with Scissors.
Faceless Janus.
Perforated Ladle.

When angered, the Poet brandishes an admonitory index finger.
This intimidates no one.
The Poet's family tree produces lemons.

Among the Poet's quips:
If you observe your world from a picture frame,
you're a portrait.
If menacing gestures obscure your view,
depart on a yet to be beaten path.
Shrines most likely won't appear, even less likely, toll collectors.

The Poet finds himself at a monument.
With an etching needle he carries for happenstance encounters,
he scratches a couplet on the plinth. (One makes one's mark
where one can.)

He observes through the forest's canopy an emulsion of admonitory clouds.
Taser at the ready, the Poet continues along his unbeaten path,
where suddenly appears a mysterious stranger.
The mysterious stranger's flared pewter nostrils suggest aggression.
As it happens, not.
The mysterious stranger is merely strange
and of no further interest.

The Poet disdains irony, nor is this a poem à clef
about laureates with anal warts.
We need to move on.

Curse

Spawn of a camel's carbuncle!
Across your dreamscape
I propose a bed
of one-inch rebar
and a concrete pour.

Harsh Words

Polyphony, like embroidery,
has no place in contumely
I mention mostly to sound fancy.

In the Prefecture of Loud

alas! alas! alas! O alas! alas! alas! alas! alas! alas! alas! O! O!
        alas! O ah me! alas! (alack!)

alas! Ah me! O woe!

alas! alas! O alas! alas! O ah me! alas! alas!

        alas! O O!

alas!

alas!
alas!

O misfortune!

Raprochement

Pick up a fallen child and its parents will thank you.
Kick it in the ass and its parents will scream.
We all breathe; even so, I'm different. For example,
I strip arrows and eat the feathers.
In a similar display of goal-driven activity,
Aviator Pring flies into history.

Incontinence & Flatulence

As to tectonic movement
or Miami Beach subsidence
or species extinction
or the Easter Rebellion,
I'm too fucking old.

Questions

What mistakes are worth repeating?

Should I forget what you probably won't ask?

What fate awaits perspective deniers in three-dimensional settings?

What kind of woods do circus bears shit in?

Who first proposed that an infinity of angels can also dance in a Petri dish?

Do conundrums, once opened, require refrigeration?

Can moonlight slide on an oily surface?

Is there room enough in a bullet hole to stash one's regrets?

When flying through a windshield should one be choosy or will any soft place do?

Can obscurantists lose their way in a fog?

Who, to his regret, took dead reckoning literally?

Streets under Bridges

Streets under bridges submit to anonymity, in states moreover of liminal anxiety:
the span might collapse, in whole or in part. It happens. No matter.
Tho its street be mysterious, quaint or merely grim,
a bridge's underbelly commands one's gaze. One stands on such a street,
taking no note of condition or direction, imagining jumpers on New Year's Eve.
I have a tooth in the oven.

Architectural Feature

An architectural feature lands on one buttress and so remains,
like a lawn jockey. Reverberations throughout the realm,
madmen slamming doors, mermen herding landlocked girls, etc.
As for you, auditing broadcasts in your dental fillings,
analysis drowns in conjecture and health in general improves.

Five O'Clock Shadows

About your sister, sincerest apologies.
Speaking of metaphor, pigeons figure, as do shadows,
at different times of the day.
Even corks taste good in a metaphorical sense.
Battleships and orchestras fall among monarchical longings,
whereas miniaturization and metaphor often satisfy budgetary demands.
Perfect masonry is in large measure metaphorical,
which is to say, identical but for the lids.

Unsubscribe

Where did it begin?
With the French-&-Indian War?
With Lafayette's arrival?
With Tocqueville's insights?
Where and however, francophilia swept the land.
Frontiersmen swooned over the merest *bonjour*
and wept at the thought of a Mansard roof.
Fluffy pensées drifted like clouds.
Marble urns cluttered the Plains.
Permitting a chevalier to cop a feel (wife, guests, etc.)
as entrée to a barbecue, he'd attend avec plaisir.
A duc required something more.

The Lemon Whistle

Buy a ticket, sign up, sneak in,
do whatever you have to do,
tell them anything, I don't care,
but don't forget to mention
the lemon whistle.

Have a Nice Day

Do you laugh when I walk into walls?
Am I as entertaining as the hangman who says
Have a nice day as he pulls the lever?

Epaulettes

Epaulettes dangle, no, not there,
not there either, O put them anywhere, I don't care!
(Ball & socket, ball & socket, winter apples!)
Also beginning, etching of drawbridge giving Mormons fits.
Also beginning, My Life in Aviation.

Savages

Savages tiptoe everywhere
as if transporting lit candelabra.

High Wire

We salute fine lines delineating nations
in their way like circus high wires.
Were I not an acrophobe, I'd celebrate cartography,
parents shielding their children's eyes.

Lettuce

Lettuce to where the waters wet,
taking care lest we squish
the spirit of the place's fish.
Lettuce float willy nilly
till lust for the other makes us silly.
What drips so as I soggy on by?
I don't give a mussel's why.
Farewell, shoals, houseboats adrift,
strabismic Pisces, reflected sky.

Zouaves

Take care not to slip on Zouaves rolling around the floor like small crystal balls.

Gnocchi

A planet beset by feet: this is a problem.
On a more intimate scale, why mine? Why yours?
As a poet I'm driven to address difficult issues.
I'm further obliged to mention diaphanous vessels
with mist-like cracks in their unlikely futures.
though I know I shouldn't, I also dream about you,
even when your cleverest thoughts sound like a bonobo
trying to pronounce gnocchi.

Fools Call This Love

At the time of the harvest moon
asterisks ripen and drop,
moonbeams penetrate skulls.
Fools call this love.
At the time of the harvest moon
fools nibble doorknobs. Lovers nibble beloveds.
Even an imagined portcullis enjoys a little lubrication.

Geront's Miscellany

Miscellany A

Odds and ends of a rueful character:

You light a cigar. He knows where you are.
Geront wants to be young!
No one gets a whiff of what he's thinking.

In the right light rust passes for gold.
It might as well be a hobby, flicking flakes.

To sour pillow with diminished returns.

Decibels draw shallow breaths,
statistics sidle up and lie.

How to plate what remains?
A fragile vessel, a promise of shards.

A closet. No windows. Make yourself at home.
Reveries jiggle sideways into what we imagine is
Macao's soapstone plaza, into a bay.
(Perhaps something else.)

Miscellany B

On perception:

Good dreams extract moisture from dry river beds.
You may find your way in, you will never find your way out.

In the confusion, our friend Sir Henry's foot.
The best dreams feature amusing teeth, sometimes gryphons gurgling
in the gryphon manner, sometimes a grandstand view of a May Day lumpen
auction. Geront reels in regrets, pins them to the back of his head
and forgets about them.

Hunting accident: strapped down like a shot elk, Geront fled west, evading
       sunup.
In the valley of partisan almonds, trees red with attached strangers (rouges
aux étrangers) remind one of astrology, which, like stones,
gets one nowhere.

Miscellany C

On aspiration:

Hang around till everything looks swanky and requires ribbons.
Geront signs his poems with shellac, old-school.
Life goes on, even in an ICU.

Well the doc says it's time to travel
Well let's have a Goat cigarette
Well I want two eggs on edge
Well I love your neck
Well I love your knees
Well let's have another Goat cigarette

On dropping in:

Seeing you through expectations, your head looks like a cup of coffee.
I'm coming over. Don't nod.

Geront embraced totems, tongues pinned to urges.
He saw himself as a river monster with voice to match, woo woo,
through unhinged jaws (just in case
something tasty turned up).

Miscellany D

Memories of puberty:

Geront recalls that desire leads young cocks to folly.
Mother looked him up and down, unwrapped the proxy,
got out the feather duster.

Soup hats! Monticello! Fat speed with sunburn lotion!
Rocky Mountains! Whore-house music! The Americano Chomp Stomp!

In an obscure corner of another world Melnick's caramel hoplites
stuff destiny into throw cushions. A whisper informs us of this behavior.
Clouds monitor disorder.

Geront was always a premature baby.
He sulked away the months anticipating adulation.

Miscellany E

On small talk:

Old age distributes miscellanies and forgets where it put them.
Geront would love to chat but his tongue, Head Cheese, is out and about.
Where is anyone's guess.

Geront encourages strangers to investigate snowdrifts.

Tio Leo taught furnishings to levitate. Remarkable dude!
Even so, when Geront reminisces it's more about
intergalactic property rights.

For each of Geront's youthful pranks a primate perished.
Primate mortality is no longer a personal matter.
Geront goes about his business with an untroubled conscience.

Nowadays one swallows disappointments for permanent storage. As a boy
who dined on cheerier fare, Geront longed for daily specials.
Insights occur in lesser number, achievements not so much, triumphs never.
Geront's manifesto begins Up Adventure! but he never goes anywhere.
The little rosewood violin just out of reach remains just out of reach.

Miscellany F

Among Geront's memories:

Little Tommy, rising from his sickbed to cheer the team onward, the players
      retrieving
their sport shovels, the umpire admonishing, Do not leave the stadium
before the bell tolls for whom, the team captain whispering,
If the phone rings, answer it.

On acuity:

Geront likes to think that snails serenade anyone willing to listen. But this is
      about
nacre and his first dress shirt. He thought he heard his buttons singing.
He was too alarmed to engage, the buttons grew weary,
silence. A moment he'd love to revisit.

A boy's feisty chihuahuas, at twice the price you'd pay
for their weight in cold cuts.

Mother climbing a tree. An unreliable memory? Geront also recalls mother
      fraternizing
with he-men on snowshoes in the 25-watt light over the bathroom mirror.
The image disperses in a swirl of dust.

Miscellany G

On travels:

Adage: The sea permits those who cross its surface short-term trails.
Sea changes: a magus drifting by in his watertight hat.

[In order to sustain this work's prosaic tone, we removed the marginally poetic
"The sea shimmers like a lace-sample catalog's wind-fluttered pages."
Obviously, the reader has no sense of this, which is why we include this
apostrophe. We can't call it a sidebar. Nor is it a footnote.]

Miscellany H

On blended impressions:

Breeze today is kind of blue. Call it synesthesia, something wrapped around a
      cane,
with shifty eyes. One thinks of immediacy, as far down the line as furnishings
for furious morons, and as always, the way of the world, even
in what one's foundering senses report as entry-level evidence. The difference?
A curd. Were this work dismissive of tone maintenance, that would have been
      turd.
And you, reader, are Geront's lubrication.

First romance:

She appeared as a meteoric hypothesis steeped in a saline solution.
A faulty recollection: competing suitors clutching bouquets, falling into a pit
Geront dug.

On preventive medicine:

In certain Spanish-speaking countries thousands in arenas go wild for
      vaccinations.
But what is this to Geront, who's taken tea in a manor house?

On death:

If one intends to write about putrefaction, (expired vitality's legacy),
one unplugs his refrigerator, pulls up a chair
and waits.

In addressing your personal or community deity, begin by enumerating
—as a convenience, let's assign third-person masculine—his missteps and
blunders, no few of which look sadistic. (Geront would have asked
for proofs of existence.)

Miscellany I

Party tricks:

Appear with a scythe. Makes them uneasy.
Or mimic an agouti. Makes them want to chuck you under the chin.

On art's limitations:

Can poetry adequately picture microbes ploppity-plopping
across weary organs, installing expiration dates?
Autumn slips on winter's ice.

On mortality:

Death, that emphatic punctuation,
hovers over inglenooks.

Nice old poets settle comfortably on lily pads and croak.
Crazy old poets brandish galvanized buckets.
Geront is eternal (or so he thought). Now he wiggles his toes in the cold flowers,
if only to know that his feet haven't wandered off.

Miscellany J

Remembrance distorts. If the spirit moves one to reminisce,
it's best to bite one's tongue. Or anything immediately available.

A kindergarten recollection:

Pinkie Stutz's spun-sugar head with its overwound mainspring,
tears resembling pecans (but tasting like tears,
which is why they cost less).

That wasn't an offer to chew on just anything.

On days abroad:

Someone or something broke Geront's heart.
Who or what he cannot recall, nor does he know where, later,
whoever or whatever relocated. "Sounding like a tortoise," okay, but why?
"A mouth like an open furnace door," okay, but why?
Had he fallen victim to the Comintern's allure? Was he scheming
with agents under a vast Bukhara supported by Macassar ebony poles,
he in English, they in glyphs? Geront retains a memory
of perfect, pearly teeth and flower-sweet breath.
Where did this angel get off to?

From the same recollection:

Geront wandered over to a busy table. Earnest people signing a treaty.
He added his signature and, would you believe it,
he acquired four hundred acres of forested hills, a lake
and an axe!

Miscellany K

On skydiving:

When dropping swiftly from a height a longing for farmlands
is in no way wistful when you consider a haystack's absorbency.
One's ankle-length teardrops commemorate youth.

A love letter recalled:

Beloved, why did your mouth leave so many holes? You said you love me
but you left me full of holes. Your perfect breasts' parabolas
bedevil my senses. I sit here at our favorite table listening to Florian
milking to death the baleful czardas Woodsman at Sea.

On recollection of table-talk:

Geront: "I really like I here."
Father: "I really like it here too."
Mother enters and sits. "So what's the story?"

On military service:

Mess sergeant Xu upon arising: "I just wok up."
A subaltern at an open window plays a bamboo flute.
"We come as friends, we adore your food and wine,
but all these creepy gods of yours, your women's
stupid jug handles! We have to kill you!

Miscellany L

Environmental issues:

The sand dollar's low expectations (nature getting by on a budget):
Rather than indulging in a Russified despair, Geront lingers at a traffic
circle contemplating the sand dollar as any fool's plaything.
They say we're defined by our lineaments and
all too often stinky liniments.

On Islamophilia:

Bedouin music's first thought: I wonder where I'll be next. If you listen
to an empty oil drum you'll be asking similar questions. (This works
best with your ears just inside the rim.)

On presumptuousness:

A to Z, they say they are clever. We shall see.

Fire something into the sky. Try not to miss. If you do, which is likely,
settle for a cruise on Cleopatra's barge.

Miscellany M

On recalling a test question:

A man drives a certain car a certain distance at a certain speed. He regrets
the personal gas he inflicts on the leather upholstery. No worries,
it's a stolen car. He also knows that ostrich farms are largely
given over to ashrams. While ostriches still exist in numbers, many fewer
have plucked rumps. As to cuisine, to scramble ostrich eggs
requires a floor-standing mixer. Ostrich flesh does not taste like
chicken. In the main ostriches enjoy untroubled passings.

Miscellany N

On disappointment:

Geront thought she was his snug harbor.
Like a paper boat in a child's bath, one had best be poised for different vistas.
Fate lifts its large, fruity nose, sniffs and sighs.

A porphyry sarcophagus. Wispy clouds of expired desires.
Out of nowhere, grimacing Death. Geront notes
the Dark Angel's dentures.

Miscellany O

On exploring caves:

Having entered through the Ingrates' Ingress, Geront looks for the Egrets' Egress.
In his fumblings (the cave is dark) he comes upon a mailbox—a mailbox
in a cave! That's crazy! And out tumbles a deed to a gold mine!
Finders keepers, losers weepers. The deed's embossed calligraphy is
especially attractive. Excellent quality paper too. Later that morning, in the
       shade
of the cave-keeper's cottage, Geront eats his bagged lunch. None of this
       happened.
Nor did Geront drag a lathe across a kitchen floor, nor did a monument
step off its pedestal.

O bonemeal! O maniacs! Restive livestock on Geront? Thanks, no!
He hopes to die blemish free. He once was as beautiful as a sea-grass carafe.
He could tell time by sniffing the air.

Miscellany P

Jerry:

So, tell me, Jerry, is this your first visit? Are you aware that the sea is claiming your valuables? Are you aware that the specter of the rose is working its way along your leg? Have you made other arrangements?

Jerry, if you put your mind to it even your soul can raise an erection.

Miscellany Q

On foreplay:

Geront's love nips at his heels, strangers tap on his head with teaspoons.
Where to turn?

Geront asks, What was I to her, a door through which one pitches house pets
at anti-vivisectionists in summer from the freezer? Had he wished it,
Geront could have buttered her up. He chose rather a still life in an elaborate
        frame,
where she reclines uneasily next to a memento mori.

Geront observes a couple sharing a dish of spumoni.
They look just like bison! We withdraw to a more rewarding longer-ago
where Dante Gabriel Rosetti said, "This Geront fellow
is a font of delights."

Miscellany R

An assortment:

Geront tries to remember what drained his memory.
But he does remember what bilgewater becomes when it's neglected.

Adages:

He's not much of a friend if he clubs you with your mother, or his.

If your getaway vehicle is a cloud you lack substance.

Miscellany S

On good luck:

Geront opened an oyster enclosing a pearl he named Nation's Capitol
owing to a resemblance. He has a gift for naming—
and lucky withal.

On the good life:

Geront dined on potatoes yet more prestigious than Yukon gold.

Miscellany T

On resemblance:

Not unlike the Gobi dromedary, making sweet tinkly noises as it ambles along,
Geront was again fashioning heads, scratching them behind the ears,
igloos with hair. In glossy tights and floor-length cape,
as Captain Alternate, flying, chewing, sleeping, awake, Geront champions
whatever's to hand. Atlantis sank through no fault of his.
Space lay safe in his embrace.

Miscellany U

On grace under fire:

Pay attention to the mallet.
Look for a doorknob that works.
Find something that stands between
you and shrapnel, often mistaken for birth
day greetings.

Miscellany V

On measurements:

Geront displaces a precise measure of emptiness with a commensurately precise
    measure
of corporeality. One's being in the volumetric sense is a condition of occupancy
and, when all functions as it should, maneuverability, so ahoy, crazy girlies who
    suck toes,
and ahoy to you too, man slamming doors, and ahoy to you too also,
crevasse in waiting, where you leave Geront vertical.
May all of you prosper.

It's your turn, reader. Lay claim to a swath of land. Sitting at your attainment's
    center,
getting your palm fronds tangled, with your overseer's grand moustachio
and promising schemes, tell us how much in acres or hectares.

"I will spend the pearly early hours describing what knocked me over."

Miscellany W

On clarity:

When the murk is upon him, Geront likens his collected poems to a telephone
        directory:
whoever reads them beginning to end requires a diversion.
And in similar vein, Geront's poems are Janus-like creatures gazing at exits.
And in similar vein, punctures don't amount to much unless they're in you.
And in similar vein, Geront's personal favorite,
Landgrave Glatt-Kosher Rubs the Plumbing,
needs torque.

It's not all that transformative beyond the horizon.
You're better off where you are, behind the ice-cream cake.

A baker's-dozen thoughts, six squirming, seven rigid,
remind Geront to feed the golem.

Miscellany X

Pay for the ride or leave:

Forms enter through porosities.
Geront recognizes Animus Husbandry, a vampire.
Another, Lover, loiters under lindens, in a swarm of its own.
A third, Trepanation, is quaint, hectic, squalid, useless . . .
It doesn't care.

Miscellany Y

On might have been:

Hauling pianos through deep snow.

Flatulence ruining a perfectly lovely sunrise.

Geront falling out of a tree and a witness weeping
over his failure to see what's funny.

Cossacks jumping into a vat of chicken paprikash
on having been informed that Jews
are on the warpath.

Miscellany Z

With Old Age Comes Encapsulated Wisdom:

A welcoming smile absent lips
more resembles a raptor's snarl.

The wise man does not bring
an umbrella to a duel.

When a poet exits his mother's womb
library lions awaken.

As surprises go,
little compares with reincarnation.

Only somnambulists know how to do the Sleepybug,
which they forget when they awaken.

Now that their feathers are less often sought,
bird complaints are fewer.

Maintain a hopeful demeanor
until you know better.

When visitors remark, What a terrible view,
mention that it's also vindictive.

If your parents reside in a crate,
consider a footloose future.

A fig on a neck cannot compare
to an armpit mango.

Diaphanous fops sheltering from illusory thugs
behind phantom doors—I'll believe it when I can't see it.

If your lover appears wearing a cuirass
prepare for difficult moments.

Never be so exuberant
that you spill expensive wine on the cat.

Thoughts that taste like chicken
require condiments.

One better detects one's flaws
downwind.

For best results simmer an enemy
in the sweat of a day's wonder-working.

Fortuna stops at the pavement's edge
where Chaos takes over.

Create interest by declaring yourself
more up to date than you were last year.

When your hand explores the wrong beloved,
pitons occur where no one climbs.

If a philosopher's eyes cloud over,
anticipate metaphysical rain.

(None of this is true. Call the police.)

Mike Silverton is the author of *Trios* (Sagging Meniscus, 2023) and *Anvil on a Shoestring* (Sagging Meniscus, 2022). He is a regular contributor to the quarterly literary journal *Exacting Clam*.

His poetry appeared in the late '60s and '70s in numerous periodicals and anthologies. He produced poetry readings for The New School for Social Research, New York's municipal radio station, WNYC, and Pacifica Radio's WBAI, KPFA, and KPFK. One glaring regret: Mike had arranged to record Frank O'Hara on the week in which he was killed, fateful weekend intervening, by a dune buggy.

Mike's music writing, centering on modernist classical, has appeared in *Fanfare*, his own *LaFolia.com*, and elsewhere. He has also reviewed high-end audio hardware for *Fanfare*, *The Absolute Sound* and *The StereoTimes.com*.

In early 2002, he and his wife Lee relocated to an 1842 house and barn in Midcoast Maine, where he indulged an interest in assemblage of an etiolated Dada persuasion, resulting in several works in a group show at The Center for Maine Contemporary Art in Rockport, and a one-man show at Belfast's Aarhus Gallery.

www.ingramcontent.com/pod-product-compliance
Lightning Source LLC
Chambersburg PA
CBHW020216090426
42734CB00008B/1103